Standin' Tall®

with

LOVE

by
Janeen Brady

Script Co-Authored
by Diane Woolley

Series Includes

1. Obedience
2. Honesty
3. Forgiveness
4. Work
5. Courage
6. Happiness
7. Gratitude
8. Love ✶
9. Service
10. Cleanliness
11. Self-Esteem
12. Dependability

®

Printed in the United States of America.

Hello friends. Today we're going to do something different, and we'll need crayons and paper. If you listeners turn off the tape recorder we'll wait while you get yours.

CHILDREN: We're ready. I have my crayons and paper. Now what do we do?

When the music starts I want you to draw a picture of love.

CHILDREN: A picture of love? What does love look like? What color is love?

Oh, there are many different ways to draw love. Close your eyes, and I'm sure you'll think of something. There's the music; now you can draw your picture of love.

CHILDREN: I'm done. Here's mine. That wasn't so hard.

They're beautiful, and each picture is different.

★ **Teacher, look at mine.**

Yes, Robbie, let's look at yours.

CHILD: It's a dog; it has a tail.

Robbie, tell us about your dog.

★ **I got him for my birthday.**

CHILDREN: Hey, what's going on? Something's pulling me. Oh, what is it? We're in Robbie's picture.

★ **Yeah, and here comes Duke.**

CHILDREN: Here, fella! Come on, big boy!

CHILD: Robbie, he went right to you!

★ **I guess that's 'cause he's my dog.**

I'm the one who takes him dinner;
I'm the one who teaches him tricks.
I'm the one he likes to run with;
I'm the one whose finger he licks.
I'm the one who gets to bathe him;
I'm the one who scratches his ear.
I'm the one who cleans his yard;
And I'm the one he likes to be near.

Because he's my responsibility, (your responsibility),
My responsibility, (your responsibility),
He's my personal D-O-G,
And that's quite a responsibility.

I'm the one who bought his collar;
I'm the one who closes the gate.
I'm the one who paints his dog house;
I'm the one who washes his plate.
I'm the one who takes him camping;
I'm the one who sees that he's fed.
I'm the one, the only one,
Who ever lets him sleep in my bed.

DUK

CHILDREN: We're out of the picture. Something brought us back.

Did you learn anything?

CHILD: We learned that love means being responsible.

Good. Let's all say it together.

CHILDREN: Love means being responsible. The more you do for your dog, the more you love him. And the more he loves you. And the love just gets bigger and bigger.

Yes, it does. There's no end to love. Children, when you hear the special chimes, stop the recorder and do something responsible that shows love, like feeding your pet or putting away your toys.

CHILDREN: We did it.

I'm proud of you. Andrea, let's look at your picture.

CHILDREN: It's round like a ball. It's green and blue. What is it Andrea?

★**It's the world.**

CHILD: Look, it's getting bigger.

Scoot your chairs back!

CHILDREN: It's filling the whole room. It's going to break the walls. It better stop.

EARTH: I am the earth. Andrea, please step forward.

★**Ye . . . ye . . . yes, Mr. Earth.**

EARTH: Why did you choose me for your picture of love?

★**Because I think you're beautiful. I love your green grass and flowers.**

EARTH: I wish everyone loved me.

CHILDREN: Don't cry, Mr. Earth. Make him stop. Is there anything we can do? Please tell us what's wrong.

EARTH: Too many people don't care any more. They pollute my streams and sky, and my animals and fish can't live. They scatter their garbage in my forests and along my highways, so instead of keeping me beautiful, they make me ugly.

CHILDREN: But we don't do that! No, we don't!

★**I've picked up other people's papers they've left behind.**

EARTH: You have?

★**Oh yes, because I care about you. I want to keep you beautiful.**

EARTH: I'm glad I met you. I wasn't sure anyone cared any more. But with people like you, I think maybe I'll make it. Thank you, Andrea, for loving me.

Mister Earth, I love you, Mister Earth, I love you
In the cold old winter when you're covered with ice,
Love your springtime showers and your summer flowers,
Your golden autumns are especially nice.
Mister Earth, I love you, Mister Earth, I love you
When the morning sun comes rolling up in the sky,
Love your days how they glisten, your nights when we listen
To the hush while we're watching the moon flying high.

Mister Earth, I love you, Mister Earth, I love you,
Love the big blue sky; I love the feel of the land,
Love the wind in motion and to smell the ocean,
To see a rainbow and to run in the sand.
Mister Earth, I love you, Mister Earth, I love you,
Though they say you're old, to me you'll always be new.
And with gifts you surround us to bless and astound us
With the wonder, the magic, the beauty of you.

CHILDREN: He's shrinking. He's just a picture again. But I think I see a smile.

Now what have you learned?

CHILDREN: Love means caring. And when we take good care of something we love it more. It's like magic.

Almost. What could you do to show you care?

CHILDREN: Water a flower. Pick up some papers.

You're thinking, and it's time to do a caring thing right now.

What did you draw, Steven?

★ **I drew pictures of my friends.**

What a lot of friends you have!

★ **This one lives next door, and this one's in my class. And that's Mr. Tuckett; he works at our store.**

How do all these people know they're your friends?

★ **Because I'm nice to them.**

One time some kids at school hurt another kid.
They were being cruel, called him names, made him cry.
But I told him not to even listen,
And I'd be his friend, I'd be his friend.

Because I love him, and that's what you do when you love somebody.
I love him; what else can you do when you love somebody?
I love him, and try to remember that he's somebody.
'Cause if we don't have love,
Well, then we don't have anything at all.

One day right nearby, saw a little girl
And I heard her cry, lost her coat, couldn't find it.
So I told her we'd go look together,
And she could share mine, she could share mine.

Because I love her, and that's what you do when you love somebody.
I love her; what else can you do when you love somebody?
I love her, and try to remember that she's somebody.
'Cause if we don't have love,
Well, then we don't have anything at all.

We couldn't talk about love if we didn't talk about friends. Did you do something nice today for someone who needed a friend? Were you kind? I hope so.

Oh, Wendy, what a pretty picture!

★**It's my sister. She got married.**

CHILDREN: I went to a wedding once; I was a flower girl. We're shrinking. We're getting smaller and smaller. Hey, my feet are stuck! Mine, too!

Children, I believe we're on top of a wedding cake.

CHILD: Maybe we're the decorations.

There are the bride and groom.

CHILD: Look, he's going to kiss her! Isn't it romantic? It's a special kind of love.

A very special kind of love.

♪♪ There's a special kind of love that makes a family
There's no doubt about it.
There's a special kind of love,
And there's no family can get by without it.
Every father and mother, each sister and brother,
And each tiny baby (and maybe more) depend upon that

Special kind of love that makes a family
And holds it together.
For that special kind of love can see a family
Through all kinds of weather.
And when you grow up, as you're bound to do,
That special kind of love will be waiting for you.
Then you can make a.home where all your dreams come true
With that special kind of love.

CHILD: I have a daddy, but he doesn't live with us.

CHILD: My dad doesn't live with us either.

All families are different. Some children live with just their father or mother, some live with their grandparents.

I live at one house with my mother;
It's strange, but my dad lives at another.
I don't get to see him every day
Makes me kind of sad.
But there's one thing I know anyway
He's a special dad.

Still we have love. Still we have love.
Still we have love. Still we have love.

Sometimes he visits me on weekends;
That's when we talk and get to be friends.
But my mom is always here with me;
She's my favorite pal.
So it's true we're still a family
And I know somehow

Still we have love. Still we have love.
Still we have love. Still we have love.

Ours is a different kind of family,
But it's a special one as can be.
Everybody's different anyway,
Every face and name.
But in spite of all the differences
One thing's still the same.

Still we have love. Still we have love.
Still we have love. Still we have love.

CHILD: Does love mean families?

I think it does.

★**I have an idea. Let's write a love-note for a person in our family.**

CHILD: And put it in a special place, like under their pillow.

How exciting! Let's write our love-note after our tape is finished. And right now I know something else we can do. When you hear the special chime turn off the recorder, run and find someone in your family, give that person a big hug and say "I love you."

★**I like love. It makes me feel all glowing inside, kind of like sunshine.**

Love is probably the greatest thing in the whole universe. It makes everything else have meaning. Everyone needs to be loved, and everyone needs to love. Allison, what a beautiful picture! Will you tell us about it?

HOME
SWEET
HOME

★ **This is a picture of God.**

CHILD: Oh, is that what God looks like?

★ **I don't know, but that's how I feel when I think about him.**

God has the greatest love of all. He loves everything and everyone. He loves Robbie's dog, and the world, and people, and he loves families.

★ **And he loves me, too.**

Oh, yes, he does. He loves each one of us.

Whenever love is in the air
I always feel like God is there.
When others all are nice to me
I hope that maybe God can see.
Where gentleness and peace are found,
I think that God is smiling down.
And when I pray and feel him near
I think that maybe heaven's here.

For God is love, the greatest love we'll ever know.
Yes, God is love, the kind of love that makes you glow.
For God is love, the perfect love; he's love divine.
The kind of love that reaches out to all mankind.
For God is love. God is love.

God
is
Love

★ **If I hang my picture on my wall, then I can remember about love.**

That's a good idea. Hang your picture where everyone can see it. Now come and sit down and let's just listen for awhile.

★ **Okay. You know what this music makes me feel like doing?**

What?

★ **Drawing a picture about love just for you.**

For me?

★ **And do you know what?**

What?

★ **You're going to love it!**

Side A of each cassette contains the complete program. **Side B** repeats the same program but leaves out the lines of the main child in the story, giving the listener the chance to read along, saying aloud the missing lines and actually becoming a member of the cast. This fascinating activity helps older children with their reading and provides an excellent opportunity for development in dramatics.

Children can sing along with the songs, color the pictures and participate in still other activities as the story progresses.

A Product of BRITE MUSIC ENTERPRISES, INC.
Music recorded and engineered at Skaggs Telecommunications Service, Inc.
Dramatics and final mix by Bonneville Productions.
Illustrations by Grant Wilson / Graphic production by Whipple & Associates.
Music arranged, conducted and mixed by Merrill Jenson.